THIS BOOK BELONGS TO:

____

Read with Isabelle reading pointer included in this book.

Hi, I am Isabelle.

I am a tiny **hummingbird**.

Counting is a great exercise for my tongue!

I am excited to count my favourite things with you.

I hope you will have fun counting in **English**,

Mandarin and **French**.

One hummingbird

y ī zh ī fēng niǎo
一隻蜂鳥

Un colibri

2

Two lychees

liǎng kē lì zhī

兩 顆 荔 枝

Deux litchis

3

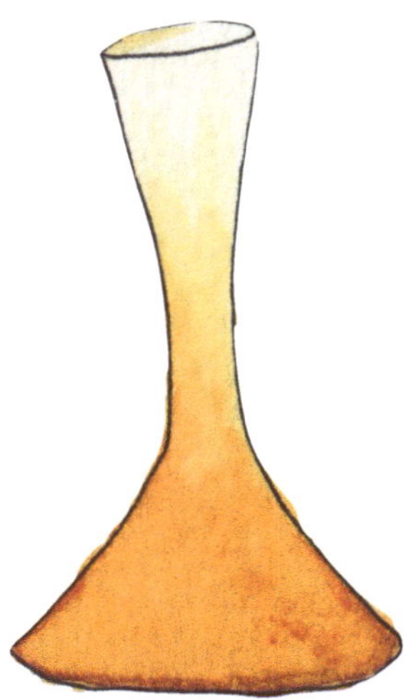

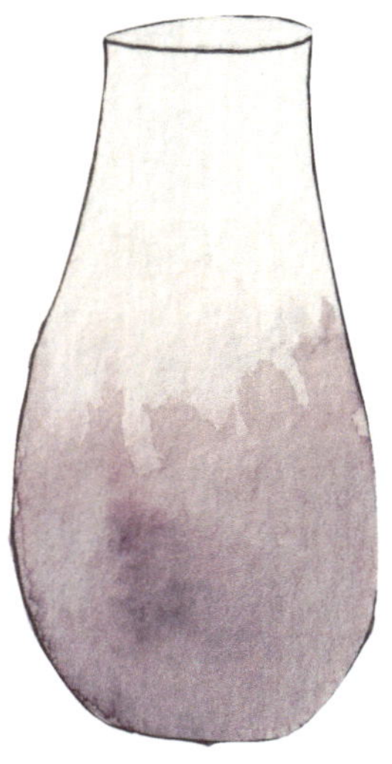

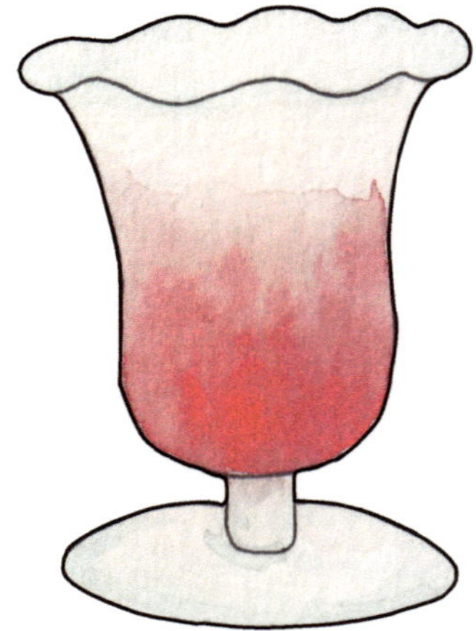

Three glasses of juice

sān bēi guǒ zhī

三杯果汁

Trois verres de jus

4

Four boxes of strawberries

sì hé cǎo méi

四盒草莓

Quatre boîtes de fraises

Five flowers

w ǔ duǒ huā

五朵花

Cinq fleurs

6

Six pies

l i ù   g è p à i
六 個 派

Six tartes

7
12
7

Seven o'clock

q ī diǎn zhōng

七點 鐘

Sept heures

8

Eight blueberries

bā lì lán méi

八粒藍莓

Huit myrtilles / bleuets

9

Nine leaves

j i ǔ **piàn** y è   z ǐ

九 片 葉 子

Neuf feuilles

10

Ten drawings

shí zhāng tú huà

十 張 圖畫

Dix dessins

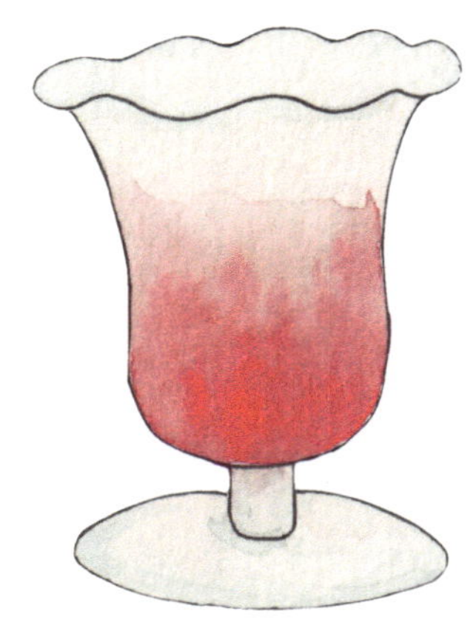

You did it!

That was excellent counting.

I am thirsty now. How about you?

Did your tongue get twisted?

Did it grow longer like mine?

I love counting and learning with you.

Author's note

Since I was young, I loved reading books ranging from fairytales, art making, poems and language learning. I dreamed of opening my own bookstore one day. My parents brightened my childhood with audio cassettes that came with books. Little did I know, years later my own children found it fascinating and enjoyed listening to those old mandarin cassettes during the Covid-19 lockdowns. This book is dedicated to my parents for their love and encouragement.

Access Free Audio Reading By The Author

Free online resources

www.jovialimagination.com

Make Isabelle reading pointers

1. Cut along the dotted line to remove this page.

2. Colour Isabelle.

3. Cut out Isabelle by following the grey lines.

4. Use Isabelle's tail, wings or mouth to point out which words you are reading.

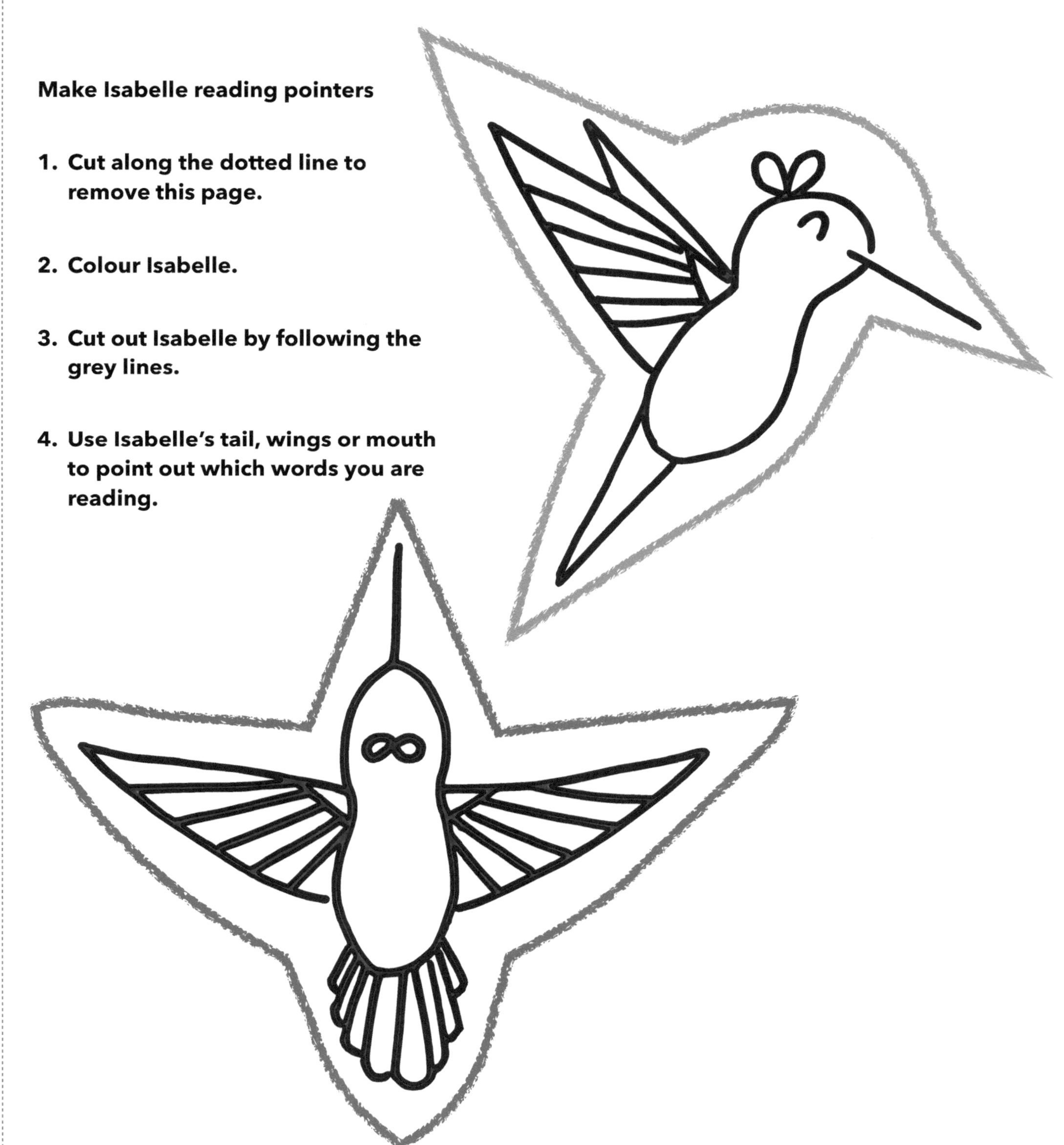

Also Available as an Ebook!

More Isabelle books coming soon!

Jovial Imagination Studio